The Lawyer's Joke Book

"There are some things a rat just won't do."

JOHN PATRICK DOLAN, *Attorney at Law*
and
DALE IRVIN, *Court Jester*

Published by Advantage, Charleston, South Carolina. Member of Advantage Media Group.

ADVANTAGE is a registered trademark and the Advantage colophon is a trademark of Advantage Media Group, Inc.

Printed in the United States of America.

ISBN: 978-1-59932-068-7
LCCN: 2008921747

Most Advantage Media Group titles are available at special quantity discounts for bulk purchases for sales promotions, premiums, fundraising, and educational use. Special versions or book excerpts can also be created to fit specific needs.

For more information, please write: Special Markets, Advantage Media Group, P.O. Box 272, Charleston, SC 29402 or call 1.866.775.1696.

INTRODUCTION

Lawyer jokes have been around since there have been lawyers. In fact, the very first lawyer to ever pass the bar was Mediocritus, who went on to invent the billable hour. People make jokes about lawyers for the same reason that dogs lick themselves…because they can. Lawyers are easy targets because everyone in America has at one time either a) hired a lawyer, b) hated a lawyer, or c) has been a lawyer. No matter what your affiliation with the legal profession is, you will enjoy this book. If you don't enjoy it, hey, sue us.

ABOUT THE COVER

The subtitle of this book is actually the punch line to one of the original jokes about lawyers. Here is that joke in its entirety.

Did you hear that they're replacing laboratory rats with lawyers? They're doing it because:

1. They are in more plentiful supply.

2. You don't get emotionally attached to them.

3. There are some things that rats just won't do.

With that out of the way, enjoy the next 100 jokes about lawyers.

*　　*　　*　　*　　*

An attorney died and found himself in heaven, but not at all happy with his accommodations. He complained to St. Peter, who told him that his only recourse was to appeal his assignment. The attorney immediately advised that he intended to appeal, but was then told that he would be waiting at least three years before his appeal could be heard. The attorney protested that a three-year wait was unconscionable, but his words fell on deaf ears.

The lawyer was then approached by Satan, who told him that he could arrange an appeal in two days, if the attorney was willing to change venue to Hell. When the attorney asked why appeals could be heard so much sooner in Hell, Satan said, "We have all of the judges."

*   *   *   *   *

Do you know what happens when a lawyer takes Viagra?

He gets taller.

*   *   *   *   *

An old man was critically ill and near death. He called his lawyer and told him in a weak voice, "I want to become a lawyer. How much is it for the express degree you told me about?"

"It's $50,000," the lawyer said. "But why? You'll be dead soon, why do you want to become a lawyer?"

"That's my business! Get me the course!"

Four days later, the old man got his law degree. His lawyer was at his bedside, making sure his bill would be paid. Suddenly the old man was racked with fits of coughing and it was clear that this would be the end. Still curious, the lawyer leaned over and said, "Please, before it's too late, tell me why you wanted to get a law degree so badly before you died?"

In a faint whisper, as he breathed his last breath, the old man said, "One less lawyer."

*   *   *   *   *

Alimony: The ransom that the happy pay to the devil.   – H. L. Mencken

*   *   *   *   *

It was a nice day at the park by the lake. Three guys were casting their lines to catch some fish and a couple was rowing in a small boat. Two crows were cruising by, eyeing for some targets to poop on. The younger of the two crows tried to show off and dove onto those three guys. Tut, tut, tut. But it went thud, thud, hitting only two of the three.

The older crow went towards the couple in the moving row boat. Tut, tut. And it went thud, hitting only one of the couple. Since this was a moving target, it didn't seem all that bad.

Then out from nowhere came this little bird, wings still wet like it had just been hatched. It dove towards those three guys. Tut, tut, tut. Thud, thud, thud. It swooped over to the row boat. Tut, tut. Thud, thud. Then a kid riding a bike came around. It flew over there. Tut. Thud. And it then rested on a tree branch.

So the two crows felt embarrassed and went over there, said, "We are impressed! Where did you learn to poop on people like that?"

The little one said, "I may be a new hatch

but I've got plenty of experience. In my former life I was a lawyer."

*　　*　　*　　*　　*

Judges, as a class, display, in the matter of arranging alimony, that reckless generosity which is found only in men who are giving away someone else's cash.

– P. G. Wodehouse

*　　*　　*　　*　　*

The scene is a dark jungle in Africa. Two tigers are stalking through the brush when the one to the rear reaches out with his tongue and licks the ass of the tiger in front. The startled tiger turns around and says, "Hey! Cut it out, already." The rear tiger says, "Sorry but I just ate a lawyer and I'm trying to get the taste out of my mouth!"

*　　*　　*　　*　　*

The judge asked the defendant to please stand. "You are charged with murdering a school teacher with a chain saw." From out in the gallery, a man shouts, "Lying bastard!"

"Silence in the court!" the judge says to the man who shouted. He turns to the defendant and says, "You are also charged with killing a paperboy with a shovel."

"Damn tightwad," the same man in the gallery blurted out.

"I said QUIET!" yelled the judge. To the defendant, "You are also charged with killing a mailman with an electric drill."

"You jackass!" the man from the gallery yelled. The judge thundered at the man in the galley, "If you don't tell me right now the reasons for your outbursts, I'll hold you in contempt!"

The man answered back, "I've lived beside that man for ten years now, but do you think he ever had a tool when I needed to borrow one?!"

*   *   *   *   *

A stingy old lawyer, who had been diagnosed with a terminal illness, was determined to prove wrong the saying, "You can't take it with you." After much thought and consideration, the old ambulance chaser finally figured out how to take at least some of his money with him when he died.

He instructed his wife to go to the bank and withdraw enough money to fill two pillow cases. He then directed her to take the bags of money to the attic and leave them directly above his bed. His plan was that when he passed away, he would reach out and grab the bags on his way to heaven.

Several weeks after the funeral, the deceased lawyer's wife, up in the attic cleaning, came upon the two forgotten pillow cases stuffed with cash.

"Oh, that darned old fool," she exclaimed. "I knew he should have had me put the money in the basement."

*   *   *   *   *

What's the difference between a lawyer and a gigolo?

The gigolo only screws one person at a time.

*   *   *   *   *

A group of Arab terrorists burst into the conference room at the Ramada Hotel where the American Bar Association was holding its Annual Convention. More than a hundred lawyers were taken as hostages.

The terrorist leader announced that, unless their demands were met, they would release one lawyer every hour.

*   *   *   *   *

A man walked into a bar with his pet alligator on a leash and asked the bartender, "Do you serve lawyers here?"

"Sure do," replied the bartender.

"Good," said the man. "Give me a beer, and I'll have a lawyer for my gator."

*   *   *   *   *

Seems there were these three professionals sitting around talking about the oldest profession. The doctor says, "Well, the Bible says that God took a rib out of Adam to make woman. Since that clearly required surgery, then the oldest profession is surely medicine."

The Engineer shakes his head and replies, "No, no. The Bible also says that God created the world out of void and chaos. To do that, God must surely have been an engineer. Therefore, Engineering is the oldest profession."

The Lawyer smiles smugly and leans discreetly forward. "Ah," he says, "but who do you think created the Chaos?"

*   *   *   *   *

It was so cold last winter ... (How cold was it?) ...... I saw a lawyer with his hands in his own pockets!

*   *   *   *   *

Hell hath no fury like the lawyer of a woman scorned.

*   *   *   *   *

A lawyer's dog, running about unleashed, beelines for a butcher shop and steals a roast from the counter.

The butcher goes to the lawyer's office and asks, "If a dog is running unleashed and steals a piece of meat from my store, do I have a right to demand payment for the meat from the dog's owner?"

"Absolutely."

"Then you owe me $8.50. Your dog was loose and stole a roast from me today."

The lawyer, without a word, writes the butcher a check for $8.50 (attorneys don't carry cash). Several days later, the butcher opens the mail and finds an envelope from the lawyer:

An invoice : Consultation........... $200.

*   *   *   *   *

How can a pregnant woman tell that she's carrying a future lawyer?

She has an uncontrollable craving for baloney.

*   *   *   *   *

The attorney was briefing his witness before calling on him to testify and said, "You must swear to tell the complete truth, do you understand?"

The witness said, "Yes, I will swear to tell the truth."

"Do you have any idea what will happen if you don't tell the truth?" the lawyer asked.

The witness looked up and responded, "I imagine our side will win."

*　　*　　*　　*　　*

Two attorneys went into a diner and ordered two drinks. Then they produced sandwiches from their briefcases and started to eat.

The owner became quite concerned and marched over and told them, "You can't eat your own sandwiches in here!"

The attorneys looked at each other, shrugged their shoulders and then exchanged sandwiches.

*　　*　　*　　*　　*

John E. Clockran (note: any similarity between the name used in this joke and a real person is strictly coincidental) was duck hunting in Montana recently, when he attempted to cross a fence into a field to retrieve a duck he had shot. A farmer suddenly pulled up in his pick-up truck, jumped out, and asked Mr. Clockran what he was doing on his property.

"Retrieving a duck that I just shot," he replied.

"That duck is on my side of the fence, so now it's mine," replied the farmer.

Mr. Clockran asked the farmer if he recognized who he was talking to.

"No," replied the farmer. "I don't know, and I don't care."

"I am John E. Clockran, famous lawyer from Los Angeles," came the reply. "And if you don't let me get that duck, I can sue you for your farm, your truck, and everything else you own. I'll leave you penniless on the street."

"Well," said the farmer, "In Montana the only law we go by is the '3 kicks law.'"

"Never heard of it," said John E.

The farmer said, "I get to kick you 3 times, and if you make it back to your feet and are able to kick me back 3 times, that duck is yours."

Clockran thought this over. He grew up in a tough neighborhood and figured he could take this old farmer. "Fair enough," he said.

So the farmer kicked John E. violently in the groin. As he was doubling over, the farmer kicked him in the face, and when he hit the ground, he kicked him hard in the ribs. Several moments later, John E. slowly made it back to his feet.

"All right, now it's my turn," said John E.

"Aw, forget it," said the farmer. "You can have the duck."

*   *   *   *   *

An attorney was sitting in his office late one night, when Satan appeared before him.

The Devil told the lawyer, "I have a proposition for you. You can win every case you try, for the rest of your life. Your clients will adore you, your colleagues will stand in awe of you, and you will make embarrassing sums of money. All I want in exchange is your soul, your wife's soul, your children's souls, your children's children's souls, the souls of your parents, grandparents, and your parents-in-law, and the souls of all your friends and law partners."

The lawyer thought about this for a moment with a puzzled face, then asked, "OK, so... What's the catch?"

*   *   *   *   *

When a person assists a criminal in breaking the law before the criminal gets arrested, we call him an accomplice. When a person assists a criminal in breaking the law after the criminal gets arrested, we call him a defense lawyer.

*   *   *   *   *

THINGS THAT SOUND DIRTY IN LAW BUT AREN'T

- "Have you looked through her briefs?"

- "He is one hard judge!"

- "Counselor, let's do it in chambers."

- "His attorney withdrew at the last minute."

- "Is it a penal offense?"

- "Better leave the handcuffs on."

- "For $200.00 an hour, she better be good!"

- "Can you get him to drop his suit?"

- "The judge gave her the stiffest one he could."

- "Think you can get me off?"

* * * * *

What's the definition of a tragedy?

A busload of lawyers crashes off a cliff and one seat is empty.

* * * * *

A truck driver frequently traveled through a small town where there was a courthouse at the side of the road. Of course, there were always lawyers walking along the road. The truck driver made it a practice to hit any pedestrian lawyers with his truck as he sped by.

One day, he spotted a priest walking along the road and stopped to give him a ride. A little further along, as he approached the town, he spotted a lawyer walking along the side of the road.

Automatically, he veered his truck towards the lawyer, but...then he remem-bered his passenger. He swerved back to the center, but he heard a "whump" and in the rear view mirror he spotted the lawyer rolling across the field.

He turned to the priest and said, "Father, I'm sure that I missed that lawyer!"

And the priest replied, "That's OK, my son, I got him with the door."

*   *   *   *   *

A lawyer died and arrived at the pearly gates. To his dismay, there were thousands of people ahead of him in line to see St. Peter.

To his surprise, St. Peter left his desk at the gate and came down the long line to where the lawyer was, and greeted him warmly.

Then St. Peter and one of his assistants took the lawyer by the hands and guided him up to the front of the line, and into a comfortable chair by his desk.

The lawyer said, "I don't mind all this attention, but what makes me so special?"

St. Peter replied, "Well, I've added up all the hours for which you billed your clients, and by my calculation you must be about 193 years old!"

*   *   *   *   *

A lawyer was visiting a farmer on business, when he stepped out of his Mercedes in the farmyard he stepped into a cow dropping. Looking down he cried, "My god I'm melting!"

*   *   *   *   *

SIGNS THAT YOU MIGHT NEED A DIFFERENT LAWYER

- The sign in front of his law office reads "Practicing Law Since 2:25 PM."

- Tries to cheer you up by saying how great you look in orange.

- Giggles hysterically at the mere mention of the term Penal Code.

- The only question he can come up with during cross-examination is, "Isn't it true that you're a lying bastard?"

- Constantly raising objections to the "vibes" he's getting from the jury.

- Every time the judge sustains one of his objections, he screams, "Yahtzee!"

- Instead of saying, "Your honor, I object," he now just rolls his eyes and says, "Whatever."

- He giggles whenever he hears the word "briefs."

- He begins his opening argument with the words, "As Ally McBeal once said…"

- You met him in prison.

- During your initial consultation he tries

to sell you Amway.

- When the prosecutors see who your lawyer is, they high-five each other.

- He tells you that he's never told a lie.

- He asks a hostile witness to "pull my finger."

- A prison guard is shaving your head.

- He places a large "No Refunds" sign on the defense table.

* * * * *

A woman and her little girl were visiting the grave of the little girl's grandmother. On their way through the cemetery back to the car, the little girl asked, "Mommy, do they ever bury two people in the same grave?"

"Of course not, dear." replied the mother, "Why would you think that?"

"The tombstone back there said, 'Here lies a lawyer and an honest man.'"

* * * * *

A lawyer defending a man accused of burglary tried this creative defense: "My client merely inserted his arm into the window and removed a few trifling articles. His arm is not himself, and I fail to see how you can punish the whole individual for an offense committed by his limb."

"Well put," the judge replied. "Using your logic, I sentence the defendant's arm to one year's imprisonment. He can accompany it or not, as he chooses."

The defendant smiled. With his lawyer's assistance he detached his artificial limb, laid it on the bench, and walked out.

* * * * *

A lawyer was on vacation in a small farming town. While walking through the streets, a car was involved in an accident. As expected a large crowd gathered. Going by instinct, the lawyer was eager to get to the injured, but he couldn't get near the car. Being a clever sort, he started shouting loudly, "Let me through! Let me through! I am the son of the victim."

The crowd made way for him. Lying in

front of the car was a donkey.

*   *   *   *   *

After years of hard work, Angie took her first vacation on a luxury cruise ship. While sitting in a deck chair, she recognized a former high school classmate, a long-lost friend from her old hometown.

She crossed the deck and shook hands with her friend and said: "Hello, Angela. I haven't seen you in years. What are you doing these days?"

"I'm practicing law," whispered Angela. "But don't tell my mother. She still thinks I'm a prostitute."

*   *   *   *   *

The post office had to recall its series of stamps depicting famous lawyers. It seems that people were confused as to which side to spit on.

*   *   *   *   *

A bus load of lawyers were driving down a country road when all of a sudden the bus ran off the road and crashed into a tree in an old farmer's field. The old farmer after seeing what happened went over to investigate. He then proceeded to dig a hole and bury the lawyers.

A few days later, the local sheriff came out, saw the crashed bus, and then asked the old farmer, "Were they all dead?"

The old farmer replied, "Well, some of them said they weren't, but you know how them lawyers lie."

*   *   *   *   *

A doctor and a lawyer in separate vehicles collided on I-95 one foggy night. The fault was questionable, but both were shaken up, and the lawyer offered the doctor a drink from a pocket flask. The doctor took the flask with a shaking hand and belted back a couple of swallows.

As the lawyer started to put the cap back on the flask the doctor asked, "Aren't you going to have one too, for your nerves?"

"Of course I am," replied the lawyer, "after

the Highway Patrol gets here."

*   *   *   *   *

A man walks into a friend and sees that his friend's car is a total-loss and covered with leaves, grass, branches, dirt and blood. He asks his friend, "What's happened to your car?"

"Well," the friend replies, "I ran into a lawyer."

"OK," says the man, "that explains the blood... But what about the leaves, the grass, the branches and the dirt?"

"Well, I had to chase him all through the park."

*   *   *   *   *

What's the difference between a lawyer and a trampoline?

You take your boots off to jump on a trampoline.

*   *   *   *   *

A gang of robbers broke into a lawyer's club by mistake. The old legal lions gave them a fight for their life and their money. The gang was very happy to escape.

"It ain't so bad," one crook noted. "We got $25 between us."

The boss screamed: "I warned you to stay clear of lawyers! We had $100 when we broke in!"

*   *   *   *   *

Shortly after a car was broadsided in a busy intersection, a good Samaritan rushed to see if anyone was hurt. He saw that the driver was dazed and bleeding. "Hang in there, lady," he said. "Are you badly hurt?"

"How the hell should I know?" she snapped. "I'm a doctor, not a lawyer."

*   *   *   *   *

What is the difference between a tick and a lawyer?

A tick falls off of you when you die.

*   *   *   *   *

Why are lawyers like nuclear weapons?

If one side has one, the other side has to get one. Once launched, they cannot be recalled. When they land, they screw up everything forever.

*   *   *   *   *

A man was sent to Hell for his sins. As he was being taken to his place of eternal torment, he passed a room where a lawyer was having an intimate conversation with a beautiful woman.

"What a rip-off," the man muttered. "I have to roast for all eternity, and that lawyer spends it with that gorgeous woman."

Jabbing the man with his pitchfork, the escorting demon snarled, "Who are you to question that woman's punishment?"

*   *   *   *   *

Lawyer's creed: A man is innocent until proven broke.

*   *   *   *   *

A lawyer is talking to his client. He says, "I have some good news, and I have some bad news."

The client says, "I could use some good news. What is it?"

"Your ex-wife is not making you pay on further inheritance."

"Great! Now what's the bad news?"

"She's marrying your father."

*   *   *   *   *

After her checkup, the young woman told her gynecologist that she was quite concerned, because every man she slept with wanted anal sex. "This may sound silly," she said, "but can I get pregnant that way?"

"It's not silly at all," the doctor replied. "Where do you think all the lawyers come from?"

*   *   *   *   *

What is black and brown and looks good on a lawyer?

A Doberman.

*   *   *   *   *

A lawyer's wife dies. At the cemetery, people are appalled to see that the tombstone reads, "Here lies Phyllis, wife of Murray, L.L.D., Wills, Divorce, Malpractice."

Suddenly, Murray bursts into tears. His brother says, "You should cry. I can't believe a mistake like this has been made on your wife's tombstone!"

Through his tears, Murray croaks, "You don't understand! They left out the phone number!"

*   *   *   *   *

A man walked into a lawyer's office and asked him what his rates were. "$50 for three questions," the lawyer replied.

"Isn't that awfully steep?" asked the man.

"Yes," the lawyer replied. "And what is your third question?"

*   *   *   *   *

What's the difference between a female lawyer and a pit bull?

Lipstick.

*   *   *   *   *

As he cross-examined the coroner, the defense attorney asked, "Before you signed the death certificate, had you taken the man's pulse?"

"No," the coroner replied.

"Oh? Did you check for breathing?"

"No."

"So when you signed the death certificate," the attorney asked with a smirk, "You had not taken any steps to make sure the man was dead, had you?"

"Let me put it this way," the badgered coroner replied. "The man's brain was sitting in a jar on my desk. But," he added, "I guess that he could still be out there practicing law somewhere."

*   *   *   *   *

What do lawyers and sperm have in common?

One in 3,000,000 has a chance of becoming a human being.

*   *   *   *   *

The two partners in a law firm were having lunch when suddenly one of them jumped up from the table and said, "I have to go back to the office. I forgot to lock the safe!"

"What are you worried about?" the other said. "We're both here."

*   *   *   *   *

This guy walked into a bar and shouted for all to hear, "Lawyers are ASSHOLES!"

A man in the back of the bar stood up and shouted back at him "I take exception to that statement and I resent it greatly!"

The first guy said "Are you a Lawyer?"

The man responded "No, I'm an asshole!"

*   *   *   *   *

What do you call 20 lawyers skydiving from an airplane?

Skeet.

*   *   *   *   *

The day after a verdict had been entered against his client, the lawyer rushed to the judge's chambers, demanding that the case be reopened. He said that he had new evidence that made a huge difference in his defense.

"What new evidence could you have?" said the judge.

The lawyer replied, "My client has an extra $10,000, and I just found out about it!"

*   *   *   *   *

What do lawyers use for birth control?

Their personalities.

*   *   *   *   *

What's the difference between a dead dog in the road and a dead lawyer in the road?

There are skid marks in front of the dog.

*   *   *   *   *

A lawyer newly hired by the Vatican was asked to join the Pope on a fishing trip. As they drifted on the still lake, the lawyer accidentally dropped an oar in the water and watched as it floated away. The Pope stepped out of the boat, walked across the water to the oar, grabbed it and walked back to the boat.

The next day at the office, a colleague asked the attorney if he had enjoyed fishing with the Pope, since it must have been a truly amazing experience.

"It was Ok," the lawyer replied, "But would you believe that guy can't swim?"

*   *   *   *   *

What do you have when a lawyer is buried up to his neck in sand?

Not enough sand.

*   *   *   *   *

How do you get a lawyer out of a tree?

Cut the rope.

*   *   *   *   *

A defendant was on trial for murder. There was strong evidence indicating guilt, but there was no corpse. In the defense's closing statement the lawyer, knowing that his client would probably be convicted, resorted to a trick.

"Ladies and gentlemen of the jury, I have a surprise for you all," the lawyer said as he looked at his watch. "Within one minute, the person presumed dead in this case will walk into this courtroom." He looked toward the courtroom door. The jurors, somewhat stunned, all looked on eagerly. A minute passed. Nothing happened.

Finally the lawyer said, "Actually, I made up the previous statement. But, you all looked on with anticipation. I therefore put to you that you have a reasonable doubt in this case as to whether anyone was killed and insist that you return a verdict of not guilty." The jury, clearly confused, retired to deliberate. A few minutes later, the jury returned and pronounced a verdict of guilty.

"But how?" inquired the lawyer. "You must have had some doubt; I saw all of you stare at the door." The jury foreman replied, "Oh, we looked, but your client didn't."

*   *   *   *   *

How do you save a drowning lawyer?

Take your foot off his head.

*   *   *   *   *

What can a goose do, a duck can't, and a lawyer should?

Stick his bill up his ass.

*   *   *   *   *

What's the difference between a lawyer and a carp?

One is a cold blooded bottom dwelling scavenger and the other is a fish.

*   *   *   *   *

Why don't sharks eat lawyers?

Professional courtesy.

*   *   *   *   *

Murphy, a dishonest lawyer, bribed a man on his client's jury to hold out for a charge of manslaughter, as opposed to the charge of murder which was brought by the state.

The jury was out for several days before they returned with the manslaughter verdict. When Murphy paid the corrupt juror, he asked him if he had a very difficult time convincing the other jurors to see things his way.

"Sure did," the juror replied, "the other eleven wanted to acquit."

*   *   *   *   *

How can you tell if a lawyer is well hung?

You can't get your finger between the rope and his neck.

*   *   *   *   *

What do you call a lawyer with an I.Q of 40?

Your Honor.

*   *   *   *   *

A man goes into a pet shop to buy a parrot. The shop owner points to three identical-looking parrots on a perch and says, "The parrot on the left costs $500."

"Why does the parrot cost so much?" asks the customer.

The owner says "Well, this parrot knows how to do legal research."

The customer then asks about the next parrot, to be told that this one costs $1,000 because it can do everything the other parrot can do plus it knows how to write a brief that will win any case.

Naturally, the increasingly startled customer asks about the third parrot, to be told that it costs $4,000. Needless to say, this begs the question, "What can it do?" To which the owner replies, "To be honest, I've never seen him do a darn thing, but the other two call him Senior Partner."

*   *   *   *   *

"You seem to have more than the average share of intelligence for a man of your background," sneered the lawyer at a witness on the stand.

"If I wasn't under oath, I'd return the compliment," replied the witness.

*   *   *   *   *

How can you tell when a lawyer is lying?

His lips are moving.

*   *   *   *   *

What's the difference between God and a lawyer?

God doesn't think He's a lawyer.

*   *   *   *   *

What's the difference between a lawyer and a hooker?

The hooker stops screwing you when you're dead.

*   *   *   *   *

A guy walks into a post office one day to see a middle-aged, balding man standing at the counter methodically placing "Love" stamps on bright pink envelopes with hearts all over them. He then takes out a perfume bottle and starts spraying scent all over them. His curiosity getting the better of him, he goes up to the balding man and asks him what he is doing.

The man says "I'm sending out 1,000 Valentine cards signed, 'Guess who?'" "But why?" asks the man.

"I'm a divorce lawyer," the man replies.

*   *   *   *   *

What do you call 100,000 lawyers at the bottom of the ocean?

A good start.

*   *   *   *   *

How do you kill a lawyer when he's drinking?

Slam the toilet seat on his head.

*   *   *   *   *

Defendant: Judge, I want you to appoint me another lawyer.

Judge: And why is that?

Defendant: Because the Public Defender isn't interested in my case.

Judge (to Public Defender): Do you have any comments on the defendant's motion?

Public Defender: I'm sorry, Your Honor. I wasn't listening.

*　　*　　*　　*　　*

What's the difference between a lawyer and a vulture?

Vultures wait until you're dead to rip your heart out.

*　　*　　*　　*　　*

Why does the law society prohibit sex between lawyers and their clients?

To prevent clients from being billed twice for essentially the same service.

*　　*　　*　　*　　*

You're trapped in a room with a tiger, a grizzly bear and a lawyer. You have a gun with two bullets. What should you do?

Shoot the lawyer. Twice.

*   *   *   *   *

Did you hear about Evel Knievel's newest stunt?

He'll attempt to jump 1,000 lawyers with a bulldozer.

*   *   *   *   *

What do you buy a friend graduating from Law School?

A Lobotomy.

*   *   *   *   *

What do you call a block of cement containing ten lawyers?

A waste of cement.

*   *   *   *   *

Where can you find a good lawyer?

In the cemetery.

*   *   *   *   *

There was this farmer who was out one day in the field and stumbled across an old lamp. The farmer brought it in the house and started cleaning it. Then a genie appeared and said, "I am here to grant you three wishes, but you have to remember that whatever you wish, every lawyer in town is going to get two of whatever you wish."

The farmer said, "That's okay." So, the farmer wished for a Porsche.

The genie said, "Every lawyer is going to get two Porsches."

He said, "That's okay."

The genie asked, "What is your second wish?"

The farmer asked for a million dollars.

The genie said, "Remember every lawyer in town is going to get two million dollars." The farmer said, "That's okay, we will all be rich."

The genie granted it, then he asked what the farmer's third wish would be. The farmer thought about it for awhile and then replied, "I wish to remove one of my testicles."

*   *   *   *   *

How do you save five drowning lawyers?

Who cares?

*   *   *   *   *

What do you do if you run over a Lawyer?

Back over him to make sure.

*   *   *   *   *

What's the difference between a lawyer and a bucket of manure?

The bucket.

*   *   *   *   *

What do you get when you cross the Godfather with a lawyer?

An offer you can't understand.

*   *   *   *   *

God decided to take the devil to court and settle their differences once and for all.

When Satan heard this, he laughed and said, "And where do you think you're going to find a lawyer?"

*   *   *   *   *

Santa Claus, the tooth fairy, an honest lawyer and an old drunk are walking down the street together when they simultaneously spot a hundred dollar bill. Who gets it?

The old drunk, of course, the other three are mythological creatures.

*   *   *   *   *

Why is it that many lawyers have broken noses?

From chasing parked ambulances.

*   *   *   *   *

Taking his seat in his chambers, the judge faced the opposing lawyers.

"So," he said, "I have been presented, by both of you, with a bribe."

Both lawyers squirmed uncomfortably.

"You, attorney Leon, gave me $15,000. And you, attorney Campos, gave me $10,000."

The judge reached into his pocket and pulled out a check.

He handed it to Leon, and stated "Now then, I'm returning $5,000, and we're going to decide this case strictly on its merits."

*   *   *   *   *

Why to lawyers wear neckties?

To keep the foreskin from crawling up their chins.

*   *   *   *   *

A lawyer was training a new intern on the practical application of law, when a farmer rushed into the office. The farmer said, "My no-good, lying, cheating, lice-infested jackal of a neighbor promised to sell me one of his cows for $2000. I paid him the money, but he won't give me the cow! I want to sue him to get my money back!"

The lawyer takes down the details of the case, then tells the farmer, "It sounds like a good case to me. We'll sue him to smithereens! Don't worry about the money!" The farmer is satisfied, and leaves.

Two hours later, another farmer rushes into the office. The second farmer claims that he sold a cow to his neighbor, but never received the $2000 he was promised. The lawyer takes down all the details of the case, and says, "It sounds like a good case to me. We can sue him. Don't worry about the money!"

After the second farmer left, the intern asked the lawyer, "That didn't seem very ethical to me. You told both of those men that you'd take their case, when you knew that they were suing each other. Then, you had the nerve to tell both of them not to worry about the money. How could you lie to them like that?"

"Lie?" asked the lawyer.

"Yeah, how can you get away with telling both of them not to worry about the money?" asked the intern.

The lawyer smiled broadly. "Nothing to it, my boy!" he said. "Neither one of them needs to worry about the money."

"Why not?"

The lawyer's smiled and said, "Simple. I'll get the money!"

*   *   *   *   *

Why are lawyers great in bed?

They get so much practice screwing people.

*   *   *   *   *

A small town prosecuting attorney called his first witness, a grandmotherly, elderly woman, to the stand in a trial. He approached her and asked, "Mrs. Jones, do you know me?"

She responded, "Why, yes, I do know you Mr. Williams. I've known you since you were a young boy. And frankly, you've been a big disappointment to me. You lie, you cheat on your wife, you manipulate people and talk about them behind their backs. You think you're a rising big shot when you haven't the brains to realize you never will amount to anything more than a two-bit paper pusher. Yes, I know you."

The lawyer was stunned. Not knowing what else to do he pointed across the room and asked, "Mrs. Williams, do you know the defense attorney?"

She again replied, "Why, yes I do. I've known Mr. Bradley since he was a youngster, too. I used to baby-sit him for his parents. And he, too, has been a real disappointment to me. He's lazy, bigoted, he has a drinking problem. The man can't build a normal relationship with anyone and his law practice is one of the shoddiest in the entire state. Yes, I know him."

At this point, the judge rapped the courtroom to silence and called both counselors to the bench. In a very quiet voice, he said with menace, "If either of you asks her if she knows me, you'll be jailed for contempt!"

*   *   *   *   *

What's the difference between a lawyer and a herd of buffalo?

The lawyer charges more.

*   *   *   *   *

What's the difference between a lawyer and a vampire?

A vampire only sucks blood at night.

*   *   *   *   *

Did you hear about the lady lawyer that dropped her briefs and became a solicitor?

*   *   *   *   *

Having just had judgement entered against him, Mr. Walters was upset to be handed his lawyer's bill.

"It says here that I have to pay you $10,000 now and $500 a month for the next five years! It's like I was buying a top-of-the-line Mercedes!"

The lawyer smiled and replied, "You are."

*   *   *   *   *

When a lawyer tells his clients he has a sliding fee schedule what he means is that after he bills you it's financially difficult to get back on your feet.

*   *   *   *   *

What's the difference between a lawyer and an orthodontist? At least you get some benefit from the orthodontist's retainer.

*   *   *   *   *

An indigent client who had been injured in an accident went looking for a lawyer to represent him without cost. One lawyer told him that he would take the case on contingency.

When the client asked what "contingency" was, the lawyer replied, "If I don't win your lawsuit, I don't get anything. If I do win your lawsuit, you don't get anything."

*   *   *   *   *

A lawyer lies dying, his partner of 40 years by his bedside.

"Jack, I've got to confess. I've been sleeping with your wife for 30 years and I'm the father of your daughter, Hillary. On top of that, I've been stealing from the firm for a decade."

"Relax," says Jack, "and don't think another thing about it. I'm the one who put poison in your martini."

*   *   *   *   *

A minister and lawyer were chatting at a party.

"What do you do if you make a mistake on a case?" the minister asked.

"Try to fix it if it's big; ignore it if it's insignificant," replied the lawyer. "What do you do?"

The minister replied "Oh, more or less the same. Let me give you an example. The other day I meant to say 'the devil is the father of liars,' but instead I said 'the devil is the father of lawyers,' so I let it go."

*   *   *   *   *

A barber gave a haircut to a priest one day. The priest tried to pay for the haircut but the barber refused saying "You do God's work." The next morning the barber found a dozen bibles at the door to his shop.

A policeman came to the barber for a haircut, and again the barber refused payment saying "You protect the public." The next morning the barber found a dozen doughnuts at the door to his shop.

A lawyer came to the barber for a haircut,

and again the barber refused payment saying "You serve the justice system." The next morning the barber found a dozen lawyers waiting for a haircut.

*　　*　　*　　*　　*

The lawyer stood before the judge only to hear that court would be adjourned for the day and he would have to return the next day.

"What for?" the lawyer yelled at the judge.

The judge, equally irked by a tedious day and the lawyer's rude treatment, roared, "Fifty dollars....contempt of court. That's why!"

Upon noticing the lawyer was checking his wallet, the judge relented. "That's all right. You don't have to pay the fine right now."

The lawyer replied, "I'm just seeing if I have enough to say three more words."

*　　*　　*　　*　　*

A farmer is arrested, accused of bestiality. Too poor to hire an attorney, the Public Defender comes to visit the farmer.

"So," the farmer says, "are you any good?"

The Public Defender responds, "Well, I'm not so good at opening arguments, and I'm not so good at summations and, well I'm not so good at anything in between."

The farmer responds incredulously, "So what are you good at?"

The attorney responds, "Well, I'm pretty good at picking juries."

The farmer, not having an alternative, throws his fate to the Public Defender.

The day of the trial arrives, and the farmer is being grilled by the Prosecuting Attorney "So, Mr. Farmer, isn't it true that the goat in question is your goat?"

"Yep, she is."

"And, Mr. Farmer, isn't it true that on the day in question you were seen out in the field having sex with your goat?"

There is silence in the courtroom, and

before the farmer can answer, over in the jury box, one juror leans over to another and whispers, "You know, a good goat will do that."

*   *   *   *   *

A witness to an automobile accident was testifying. The following exchange took place between the lawyer and the witness.

The lawyer: "Did you actually see the accident?"

The witness: "Yes, sir."

The lawyer: "How far away were you when the accident happened?"

The witness: "Thirty-one feet, six and one quarter inches."

The lawyer (thinking he'd trap the witness): "Well, sir, will you tell the jury how you knew it was exactly that distance?"

The witness: "Because when the accident happened I took out a tape and measured it. I knew some stupid lawyer would ask me that question."

*   *   *   *   *

Farmer Joe decided his injuries from the accident were serious enough to take the trucking company (responsible for the accident) to court. In court the trucking company's fancy lawyer was questioning farmer Joe. "Didn't you say, at the scene of the accident, 'I'm fine'?" said the lawyer.

Farmer Joe responded, "Well I'll tell you what happened. I had just loaded my favorite mule Bessie into the...."

"I didn't ask for any details," the lawyer interrupted, "just answer the question." "Did you not say, at the scene of the accident, 'I'm fine'!"

Farmer Joe said, "Well I had just got Bessie into the trailer and I was driving down the road...."

The lawyer interrupted again and said, "Judge, I am trying to establish the fact that, at the scene of the accident, this man told the Highway Patrolman on the scene that he was just fine. Now several weeks after the accident he is trying to sue my client. I believe he is a fraud. Please tell him to simply answer the question."

By this time the Judge was fairly interested

in Farmer Joe's answer and said to the lawyer, "I'd like to hear what he has to say about his favorite mule Bessie." Joe thanked the Judge and proceeded, "Well as I was saying, I had just loaded Bessie, my favorite mule, into the trailer and was driving her down the highway when this huge semi-truck and trailer ran the stop sign and smacked my truck right in the side. I was thrown into one ditch and Bessie was thrown into the other. I was hurting real bad and didn't want to move. However, I could hear ole Bessie moaning and groaning. I knew she was in terrible shape just by her groans. Shortly after the accident a Highway Patrolman came on the scene. He could hear Bessie moaning and groaning so he went over to her. After he looked at her, he took out his gun and shot her between the eyes. Then the Patrolman came across the road with his gun in his hand and looked at me. He said, "Your mule was in such bad shape I had to shoot her. How are you feeling?"

*   *   *   *   *

A very successful lawyer parked his brand-new Lexus in front of his office, ready to show it off to his colleagues. As he got out, a truck passed too close and completely tore off the door on the driver's side. The lawyer immediately grabbed his cell phone, dialed 911, and within minutes a policeman pulled up.

Before the officer had a chance to ask any questions, the lawyer started screaming hysterically. His Lexus, which he had just picked up the day before, was now completely ruined and would never be the same, no matter what the body shop did to it.

When the lawyer finally wound down from his ranting and raving, the officer shook his head in disgust and disbelief. "I can't believe how materialistic you lawyers are," he said. "You are so focused on your possessions that you don't notice anything else."

"How can you say such a thing?" asked the lawyer.

The cop replied, "Don't you know that your left arm is missing from the elbow down? It must have been torn off when the truck hit you."

"My God!" screamed the lawyer. "Where's my Rolex?"

*   *   *   *   *

"I have good news and bad news," a defense attorney told his client. "First the bad news. The blood test came back, and your DNA is an exact match with that found at the crime scene." "Oh, no!" cried the client. "What's the good news?"

"Your cholesterol is only 140."

*   *   *   *   *

A man walks into a bar. He sees a good looking lady sitting on a stool. He walks up to her and says – "Hi there, how's it going?" She turns to him – looks him straight in the eyes and says – "I'll screw anybody – any time – any where – your place – my place – it doesn't matter." He says – "No shit, what law firm do you work for?"

*   *   *   *   *

A local United Way office realized that it had never received a donation from the town's most successful attorney. So, the volunteer in charge of contributions called on the lawyer in hopes of persuading him to contribute. "Our research indicates that out of an annual income of more than $600,000 you give not a penny to charity. Wouldn't you like to give back to the community in some way?"

The lawyer mulled this over for a moment and replied, "First, did your research also show that my mother is dying after a long incapacitating illness, and has medical bills that are several times her annual income?"

Embarrassed, the United Way rep mumbled, "Uhh... no."

"Second, that my brother, a disabled U.S. veteran, is blind and confined to a wheelchair?"

The stricken United Way volunteer began to stammer out an apology but was cut off.

"Third, that my sister's husband died in a tragic automobile accident," the lawyer said, his voice rising in indignation, "leaving her penniless with three small children?!"

The humiliated United Way representative slumped in his chair, completely beaten, and replied simply, "I... I had no idea..."

On a roll, the lawyer cut him off one final time, "...and I don't give any money to them, so why should I give any to you?!?"

*   *   *   *   *

If you see a lawyer on a bicycle, why don't you swerve to hit him?

It might be your bicycle.

*   *   *   *   *

Why are lawyers buried 12 feet underground?

Deep down they're good.

*   *   *   *   *

The scene was a tiny mountain village in a remote section of West Virginia. An old mountaineer and his young wife were getting a divorce in the local court. But custody of the children was a problem. The mother jumped to her feet and protested to the judge that since she had brought the children into this world, she should retain custody of them.

The old mountaineer also wanted custody of the children. The judge asked for his side of the story and, after a long moment of silence, the mountaineer slowly rose from his chair and said, "Judge, when I put a quarter in a candy machine and a candy bar comes out, does it belong to me or the machine?"

*   *   *   *   *

In a traffic court of a large Midwestern city, a young lady was brought before the judge to answer for a ticket given her for driving through a red light. She explained to his honor that she was a schoolteacher and requested an immediate disposal of her case so she could get to the school on time. A wild gleam came into the judge's eye. "You're a schoolteacher, eh?" he said. "Madam, I shall realize my lifelong ambition. I've waited years to have a schoolteacher in this court. Sit down at that table and write 'I went through a red light' 500 times!"

*   *   *   *   *

A lawyer was on his deathbed in his bedroom, and he called to his wife. She rushed in and said, "What is it, honey?" He told her to run and get the bible as soon as possible. Being a religious woman, she thought this was a good idea. So she ran and got it, prepared to read him his favorite verse or something of the sort. He snatched it from her and began quickly scanning pages, his eyes darting right and left. The wife was curious and asked him, "What are you doing, honey?" He simply replied, "I'm looking for loopholes!"

*   *   *   *   *

Three paramedics were boasting about improvements in their respective ambulance team's response times. "Since we installed our new satellite navigation system," bragged the first one, "we cut our emergency response time by ten percent."

The other paramedics nodded in approval. "Not bad," the second paramedic commented. "But by using a computer model of traffic patterns, we've cut our average ERT by 20 percent."

Again, the other team members gave their congratulations, until the third paramedic said, "That's nothing! Since our ambulance driver passed the bar exam, we've cut our emergency response time in half!"

*   *   *   *   *

Two small boys, not yet old enough to be in school, were overheard talking at the zoo one day.

"My name is Billy. What's yours?" asked the first boy.

"Tommy," replied the second.

"My Daddy's an accountant. What does

your Daddy do for a living?" asked Billy.

Tommy replied, "My Daddy's a lawyer."

"Honest?" asked Billy.

"No, just the regular kind," replied Tommy.

*   *   *   *   *

Someone mistakenly left the cages open in the reptile house at the Bronx Zoo and there were snakes slithering all over the place.

Frantically, the keeper tried everything, but he could not get them back in their cages.

Finally he yelled to his co-worker, "Quick, call a lawyer!"

The co-worker responded, "A lawyer? Why??"

The zookeeper barked back, "We need someone who speaks their language!"

*   *   *   *   *

The young clerk's responsibilities included bringing the judge a hot cup of coffee at the start of every day.

Each morning the judge was enraged that the coffee cup arrived two-thirds full. The clerk explained that he had to rush to get the coffee delivered while it was still hot, which caused him to spill much of it along the way.

None of the judge's yelling and insults produced a full cup of coffee, until he finally threatened to cut the clerk's pay by one-third if he continued to produce one-third less than the judge wanted.

The next morning he was greeted with a cup of coffee that was full to the brim, and the next morning and the morning after that.

The judge couldn't resist gloating over his success and smugly complemented the clerk on his new technique.

"Oh, there's not much to it," admitted the clerk happily, "I take some coffee in my mouth right outside the coffee room, and spit it back in when I get outside your office."

*   *   *   *   *

After a trial had been going on for three days, Finley, the man accused of committing the crimes, stood up and approached the judge's bench.

"Your Honor, I would like to change my plea from 'innocent' to 'guilty' of the charges."

The judge angrily banged his fist on the desk. "If you're guilty, why didn't you say so in the first place and save this court a lot of time and inconvenience?" he demanded.

Finley looked up wide-eyed and stated, "Well, when the trial started I thought I was innocent, but that was before I heard all the evidence against me."

*   *   *   *   *

In a terrible accident at a railroad crossing, a train smashed into a car and pushed it nearly four hundred yards down the track.

Though no one was killed, the driver took the train company to court.

At the trial, the engineer insisted that he had given the driver ample warning by waving his lantern back and forth for nearly a minute. He even stood and convincingly demonstrated how he'd done it.

The court believed his story, and the suit was dismissed.

"Congratulations," the lawyer said to the engineer when it was over. "You did superbly under cross-examination."

"Thanks," he said, "but their attorney sure had me worried."

"Why's that?" the lawyer asked.

"I was afraid he was going to ask if the lantern was lit!"

*   *   *   *   *

A Case Of Defamation

A man was sued by a woman for defamation of character.

She charged that he had called her a "pig."

The man was found guilty and fined.

After the trial he asked the judge, "This means that I cannot call Mrs. Johnson a 'pig'?"

The judge said that was true.

"Does this mean I cannot call a pig 'Mrs. Johnson'?" the man asked.

The judge replied that he could indeed call a pig "Mrs. Johnson," with no fear of legal action.

*   *   *   *   *

Ben Dover and C. Howlett Fields Attorneys At Law

*   *   *   *   *

A prospective juror in a Dallas District Court was surprised by the definition of voluntary manslaughter given the panel:

"An intentional killing that occurs while the defendant is under the immediate influence of sudden passion arising from an adequate cause, such as when a spouse's mate is found in a 'compromising position.'"

"See, I have a problem with that passion business," responded one jury candidate. "During my first marriage, I came in and found my husband in bed with my neighbor. All I did was divorce him. I had no idea that I could have shot him."

She wasn't selected for the jury.

*   *   *   *   *

EPILOG

The epilog is the last part of a book that comes either before or after the appendix, the glossary, and the index. Nobody usually reads the epilog so we thought it would be a perfect place to write anything we wanted to.

We hope you enjoyed this book of lawyer jokes. Some were old, some were new, and almost all of them were in questionable taste.

ABOUT THE AUTHORS

As a California Criminal Trial Lawyer with over 30 years of courtroom experience, **John Patrick Dolan** has handled everything from traffic tickets to death penalty murder cases. Dolan is a recognized California State Bar Certified Specialist in Criminal Law and a true courtroom veteran. He is AV (highest) Martindale-Hubbell rated.

As an author, John Patrick Dolan has written twelve, best-selling books, including his classic *Negotiate like the Pros™*. He is a recognized international authority on negotiation and conflict resolution.

A communications veteran, John Patrick Dolan is a radio broadcaster and television legal news analyst appearing frequently on Fox News Channel, MSNBC, and Court TV. He has also been honored by the National Speakers Association as a member of the Professional Speakers Hall of Fame.

In addition to his professional legal experience, John Patrick Dolan serves as CEO of LawTalk™ MCLE, Inc., a continuing legal education company since 1992.

John Patrick Dolan is a native Californian. He

grew up in Huntington Beach, California..."Surf City USA." He is a life long drummer. His rock and roll band "The Wild Ones" was his passion during his younger days. His undergraduate studies at California State University Fullerton yielded a Bachelor degree in Speech Communication and Political Science. During his college years, John Patrick Dolan was recognized as a nationally ranked debater. His debating performance at one national event was described by Professor Laurence Tribe as a "Tour de Force."

John Patrick Dolan attended Western State University College of Law, from which he graduated in 1977 with a J.D. degree. During Law School he served as a law clerk and sat second chair on numerous criminal cases including two murder trials. Additionally, he supported himself during law school as a stockbroker for Merrill Lynch. Dolan passed the California Bar Exam and was sworn into practice in 1978. He is admitted to practice in California and numerous Federal jurisdictions. Additionally, he is admitted to practice before the Supreme Court of the United States of America, originally sponsored by F. Lee Bailey.

John Patrick Dolan lives in Southern California with his wife of 37 years, Irene the Queen, his daughter Andrea "A.J." and their Yorkshire Terrier, Jessie. When not involved in the practice of law, broadcasting, or professional speaking, John Patrick Dolan spends his time playing racquetball and practicing Shotokan Karate...he is a black belt!

Dale Irvin is the Professional Summarizer. As the meeting emcee, he attends conferences to listen, learn and observe. Then, he reports back to the audience in the form of a comedy monologue written on the spot. It is truly a one of a kind presentation.

Dale has also written eight books (available at www. daleirvin.com) and is a member of the Professional Speaker Hall of Fame. He can be heard weekly with John Patrick Dolan on the popular radio program LawTalk LA.

For a free humorous recap of the week's news, subscribe to Dale Irvin's Friday Funnies by visiting www.daleirvin.com, and clicking the buttons for Friday Funnies. It's the perfect way to end your work week.

For booking information call 800-951-7321.

All products can be ordered directly from www.daleirvin.com.

PRODUCTS BY
Dale Irvin

Laughter Doesn't Hurt $12.95
*Hilarious book based on Dale's popular
program of the same name.*

Laughter Doesn't Hurt – THE LIVE PERFORMANCE
DVD of Dale's laugh filled show.
DVD $20.00
Combo Special (DVD & Book) $25.00

Dale Irvin Rewrites History $12.95
*Hilarious book about real people,
historic events, and totally made up stories.*

Dale Irvin Rewrites History (2 CDs)
If you don't like to read, let Dale read the book to you.
Combo Special (CD & Book) $25.00

Outlaws Of Success $12.95
*Dale and four of his highly successful friends talk
about bending the rules without crossing the line.*
Outlaw Wisdom $12.95
Book of quotes by the Outlaws of Success.

Outlaw Combo $20.00
Both Outlaw books in one handy package.

Insurance As A Second Language $12.95
*If you sell insurance, own insurance, or can spell
insurance, you need this book. No facts, all funny.*

The Lawyer's Joke Book $9.99
*Need more copies of the book you're holding? Order
them right here.*
Add **$4.00** for shipping and handling in the US.
Please pay by check, Visa, or Mastercard.
BONUS: *Spend $50 or more and receive a free year
subscription to Funny Business, Dale's humor newsletter
that will leave you laughing six times a year.*

To order
Dale Irvin's products contact:

www.daleirvin.com

Dale Irvin
P. O. Box 302
Downers Grove, IL 60515

800-951-7321

BOOKS BY
John Patrick Dolan

Negotiate like the Pros™ $14.95
John Patrick Dolan's Classic

GenderSense™ $19.99
Gender and Negotiation

World Class Negotiation™ $29.99
International and Intercultural

Lawyers Quotes™ $9.95
Uplifting Comments on the Law

The Lawyer's Joke Book™ $9.99
"There Are Some Things a Rat Just Won't Do"

The Lawyer's Joke Book™ Card Deck $9.95

The Outlaws of Success™ $12.95
Bending the Rules Without Crossing the Line

Outlaw Wisdom™ $12.95
Quotes by the Outlaws of Success

Movers, Shakers and Change Makers™ .. $32.95
How to Get Going and Keep Going

Leadership Strategies™ $32.95
Strategic Ideas for Success

Negotiate like the Pros™ $79.95
Classic 6 CD Album

Negotiate like the Pros™ DVD—
6 CD Set $199.00

LawTalk Quotations About Lawyers $9.95

Add **$4.00** S/H per book + applicable sales tax